© 2024 Al Kal
All rights reserved.
No applicable part of this publication may be reproduced, stored in a retrieval system, or transmitted, in any form or by any means, electronic, mechanical, photocopying, or otherwise, without prior written permission from the copyright holder.

"More Baby Animal Names"
ISBN Hardcover: 979-8-9892051-3-4

Published by: ImagineHouse

For permissions, inquiries, or feedback, please contact:
ImagineHousePubs@gmail.com

First Edition: 2024
Printed in USA

A baby chicken is called a chick.
Chicks have soft, fluffy feathers.

Un pollo bebé se llama pollito.
Los pollitos tienen plumas suaves y esponjosas.

A baby raccoon is called a **kit**.

Raccoon **kits** cannot see or hear during the first few weeks of their lives.

Una mapache bebé se llama **cría de mapache**.

Las **crías de mapache** no pueden ver, ni oír durante las primeras semanas de vida.

A baby squirrel is also called a kit.

Squirrel kits can climb trees just two months after they are born.

Una ardilla bebé se llama cría de ardilla.

Las crías de ardilla pueden trepar a los árboles en sólo dos meses después de nacer.

A baby tiger is called a cub.

Cubs like to wrestle and play.

Un tigre bebé se llama cachorro de tigre.

A los cachorros de tigre les gusta luchar y jugar.

A baby hippo is called a calf.

A hippo calf is born under water.

Una hipopótamo bebé se llama ternera.

Las terneras nacen bajo el agua.

A baby pig is called a **piglet**.

Piglets like to dig with their noses.

Una cerda bebé se llama **lechóna**.

A las **lechonas** les gusta cavar con la nariz.

A baby goat is called a kid.

Kids are excellent climbers and jumpers.

Una cabra bebé se llama chiva.

Las chivitas son excelentes escaladoras y saltadoras.

A baby llama is called a cria.

Crias like to explore and play with other llamas.

Una cabra bebé se llama chiva.

Las chivitas son excelentes escaladoras y saltadoras.

A baby grasshopper is called a **nymph**.

Nymphs shed their skin to grow.

Una saltamontes bebé se llama **ninfa**.

Las **ninfas** cambian de piel para crecer.

A baby otter is called a pup.

Otter pups have special fur that helps them float.

Una nutria macho bebé se llama crío de nutria.

Los críos de nutria tienen un pelaje especial para ayudarlos a flotar.

A baby koala is called a joey.

A joey stays in its mother's pouch for six months after it is born.

Un koala bebé se llama joey.

Los joeys permanecen en la bolsa de su madre durante seis meses después de nacer.

A baby zebra is called a foal.

Zebra foals recognize their mother by her stripes.

Una cebra bebé se llama potra.

Las potras reconocen a su madre por sus rayas.

A baby monkey is called an infant.

Infants learn by copying their parents and other monkeys.

Un mono bebé se llama monito.

Los monitos aprenden imitando a sus padres y a otros monos.

Every animal has a name.
Every person has a name.

What's *your* name?

Cada animal tiene un nombre.
Cada persona tiene un nombre.

¿Cómo *te* llamas?

Acknowledgements

Many thanks once again to Ana Elena for the translations!

I'd also like to thank all the bookstore and library staff I have had the pleasure of meeting and learning from. You make me want to keep writing and creating.

www.ingramcontent.com/pod-product-compliance
Lightning Source LLC
Chambersburg PA
CBHW061402010526
44119CB00010B/239